GW01418713

What Peace Means

by Henry Van Dyke

I

Peace in the Soul

Peace I leave with you: my peace I give unto you.—ST. JOHN 14:27.

―――――――――――――――――――――――――――――

Peace is one of the great words of the Holy Scriptures. It is woven through the Old Testament and the New like a golden thread. It inheres and abides in the character of God,—

> "The central peace subsisting at the heart
> Of endless agitation."

It is the deepest and most universal desire of man, whose prayer in all ages has been, "Grant us Thy Peace, O Lord." It is the reward of the righteous, the blessing of the good, the crown of life's effort, and the glory of eternity.

The prophets foretell the beauty of its coming and the psalmists sing of the joy which it brings. Jesus Christ is its Divine Messiah, its high priest and its holy prince. The evangelists and prophets proclaim and preach it. From beginning to end the Bible is full of the praise of peace.

Yet there never was a book more full of stories of trouble and strife, disaster and sorrow. God Himself is revealed in it not as a calm, untroubled, self-absorbed Deity, occupied in beatific contemplation of His own perfections. He is a God who works and labours, who wars against the evil, who fights for the good. The psalmist speaks of Him as "The Lord of Hosts, strong and mighty in battle." The Revelation of St. John tells us that "There was war in Heaven; Michael and his angels fought against the dragon." Jesus Christ said: "I came not to send peace, but a sword."

It is evident, then, that this idea of "peace," like all good and noble things, has its counterfeit, its false and subtle versary, which steals its name and its garments to deceive and betray the hearts of men. We find this clearly taught in the Bible. Not more earnestly does it praise true peace than it denounces false peace.

There is no peace, saith the Lord, unto the wicked (Isaiah 48:22).

For they have healed the hurt of the daughter of my people slightly, saying, Peace, peace; when there is no peace (Jer. 8:11).

If thou hadst known, even thou, at least in this thy day, the things which belong unto thy peace! but now they are hid from thine eyes (St. Luke 19:42).

For to be carnally minded is death; but to be spiritually minded is life and peace (Romans 8:6).

There never was a time in human history when a right understanding of the nature of true peace, the path which leads to it, the laws which govern it, was more necessary or more important than it is to-day.

The world has just passed through a ghastly experience of war at its worst. Never in history has there been such slaughter, such agony, such waste, such desolation, in a brief space of time, as in the four terrible years of conflict which German militarism forced on the world in the twentieth century. Having seen it, I know what it means.

Now we have "supped full with horrors." We have had more than enough of that bloody banquet The heart of humanity longs for peace, as it has always longed, but now with a new intensity, greater than ever before. Yet the second course of war continues. The dogs fight for the crumbs under the peace-table. Ignorant armies clash by night. Cities are bombarded and sacked. The barbarous Bolsheviki raise the red flag of violence and threaten a war of classes throughout the world.

You can never make a golden age out of leaden men, or a peaceful world out of lovers of strife.

Where shall peace be found? How shall it be attained and safeguarded? Evidently the militarists have assaulted it with their doctrine that might makes right. Evidently the pacifists have betrayed it with their doctrine of passive acceptance of wrong. Somewhere between these two errors there must be a ground of truth on which Christians can stand to defend their faith and maintain their hope of a better future for the world.

Let me begin by speaking of *Peace in the Soul*. That is where religion begins, in the heart of a person. Its flowers and fruits are social. They are for the blessing of the world. But its root is personal. You can never start with a class—conscious or a mass—conscious Christianity. It must begin with just you and God.

Marshal Joffre, that fine Christian soldier, said a memorable thing about the winning of the war: "Our victory will be the fruit of individual sacrifice." So of the coming of peace on earth we may say the same: it will be the fruit of the entrance of peace into individual hearts and lives.

A world at war is the necessary result of human restlessness and enmities. "From whence come wars and fightings among you? Come they not hence, even of your lusts, that war in your members?" Envy, malice, greed, hatred, deceit,—these are the begetters of strife on earth.

A world at peace can come only from the cooperation of peaceful human spirits. Therefore we must commence to learn what peace is, by seeking it in our souls through faith.

Christ promised peace to His disciples at the Communion in that little upper room in Jerusalem, nineteen hundred years ago. Evidently it was not an outward but an inward peace. He told them that they would have a lot of trouble in the world. But He assured them that this could not overcome them if they believed in Him and in His Father God. He warned them of conflict, and assured them of inward peace.

What are the elements of this wondrous gift which Christ gave to His disciples, and which He offers to us?

I. First, the peace of Christ is the peace of being divinely loved. Nothing rests and satisfies the heart like the sense of being loved. Let us take as an illustration the case of a little child, which has grown tired and fretful at its play, and is frightened suddenly by some childish terror. Weeping, it runs to its mother. She takes the child in her arms, folds it to her breast, bends over it, and soothes it with fond words which mean only this: "I love you." Very soon the child sinks to rest, contented and happy, in the sense of being loved. "Herein is love, not that we loved God, but that he loved us, and sent his Son to be the propitiation for our sins." In Jesus Christ God is stretching out His arms to us, drawing us to His bosom, enfolding us in the secret of peace. If we believe in Jesus Christ as the Son of God, He makes us sure of a Divine affection, deep, infinite, inexhaustible, imperishable. "For God so loved the world, that he gave his only begotten Son, that whosoever believeth in him should not perish, but have everlasting life." God, who "spared not his dearly-beloved Son, but delivered him up for us all, how shall he not with him also freely give us all things?" "Nothing shall be able to separate us from the love of God, which is in Christ Jesus our Lord."

II. The Christian peace is the peace of being divinely controlled. The man who accepts Jesus Christ truly, accepts Him as Master and Lord. He believes that Christ has a purpose for him, which will surely be fulfilled? work for him, which will surely be blessed if he only tries to do it. Most of the discords of life come from a conflict of authorities, of plans, of purposes. Suppose that a building were going up, and the architect had one design for it, and the builder had another. What perplexity and confusion there would be! How ill things would fit! What perpetual quarrels and blunders and disappointments! But when the workman accepts the designer's plan and simply does his best to carry that out, harmony, joyful labour, and triumph are the result. If we accept God's plan for us, yield to Him as the daily controller and director of our life, our work, however hard, becomes peaceful and secure. No perils can frighten, no interruptions can dishearten us.

Not many years ago some workmen were digging a tunnel, when a sudden fall of earth blocked the mouth of the opening. Their companions on the outside found out what had happened, and started to dig through the mass of earth to the rescue. It was several hours before they made their way through. When they went in they found the workmen going on with their labour on the tunnel. "We knew," said one of them, "that you'd come to help us, and we thought the best way to make time pass quick was to keep on with the work." That is what a Christian may say to Christ amid the dangers and disasters of life. We know that He will never forsake us, and the best way to be at peace is to be about His business. He says to us: "As the Father sent me, even so send I you."

III. The Christian peace is the peace of being divinely forgiven.

"In every man," said a philosopher, "there is something which, if we knew it, would make us despise him." Let us turn the saying, and change it from a bitter cynicism into a wholesome truth.

In every one of us there is something which, if we realize it, makes us condemn ourselves as sinners, and hunger and thirst after righteousness, and long for forgiveness.

It is this deep consciousness of sin, of evil in our hearts and lives, that makes us restless and unhappy. The plasters and soothing lotions with which the easy-going philosophy of modern times covers it up, do not heal it; they only hide it. There is no cure for it, there is no rest for the sinful soul, except the divine forgiveness. There is no sure pledge of this except in the holy sacrifice and blessed promise of Christ, "Son, daughter, thy sins are forgiven thee, go in peace."

Understand, I do not mean that what we need and want is to have our sins ignored and overlooked. On the contrary, that is just what would fail to bring us true rest. For if God took no account of sins, required no repentance and reparation, He would not be holy, just, and faithful, a God whom we can adore and love and trust.

Nor do I mean that what we need is merely to have the punishment of sins remitted. That would not satisfy the heart. Is the child contented when the father says, "Well, I will not punish you. Go away"? No, what the child wants is to hear the father say, "I forgive you. Come to me." It is to be welcomed back to the father's home, to the father's heart, that the child longs.

Peace means not to have the offense ignored, but to have it pardoned: not to the punishment omitted, but to have separation from God ended and done with. That is the peace of being divinely forgiven,—a peace which recognizes sin, and triumphs over it,—a peace which not merely saves us from death but welcomes us home to the divine love from which we have wandered.

That is the peace which Christ offers to each one of us in His Gospel. We need it in this modern world as much as men and women ever needed it in the old world. No New Era will ever change its meaning or do away with its necessity. Indeed, it seems to me that we need this old-fashioned religion to-day more than ever.

We need it for our own comfort and strength. We need it to deliver us from the vanity and hollowness, the fever and hysteria of the present age. We need it to make us better soldiers and workers for every good cause. Peace is coming to all the earth some day through Christ. And those who shall do most to help Him bring it are the men and women to whom He gives Peace in the Soul.

II

Peace on Earth Through Righteousness

And the work of righteousness shall be peace: and the effect of righteousness quietness and confidence forever.—ISAIAH 32:17.

fter we have found peace in our own souls through faith in God and in His Son, Jesus Christ our Saviour, if our faith is honest, we must feel the desire and the duty of helping to make peace prevail on earth.

But here we are, in a world of confusion and conflict. Darkness and ignorance strive against light. Evil hates and assaults good. Wrong takes up arms against right. Greed and pride and passion call on violence to defeat justice and enthrone blind force. So has it been since Cain killed Abel, since Christ was crucified on Calvary, and so it is to-day wherever men uphold the false doctrine that "might makes right."

The Bible teaches us that there is no foundation for enduring peace on earth except in righteousness: that it is our duty to suffer for that cause if need be: that we are bound to fight for it if we have the power: and that if God gives us the victory we must use it for the perpetuation of righteous peace.

In these words I sum up what seems to me the Christian doctrine of war and peace,—the truth that in time of war we must stand for the right, and that when peace comes in sight, we must do our best to found it upon justice. These two truths cannot be separated. If we forget the meaning of the Christian duty to which God called us in the late war, all our sacrifice of blood and treasure will have been in vain. If we forget the watchword which called our boys to the colours, our victory will be fruitless. We have fought in this twentieth century against the pagan German doctrine of war as the supreme arbiter between the tribes of mankind. They that took the sword must perish by the sword. But in the hour of victory we must uphold the end for which we have fought and suffered,—the advance of the world towards a peaceful life founded on reason and justice and fair-play for every man.

So there are two heads to this sermon. First, the indelible remembrance of a righteous acceptance of war. Second, the reasonable hope of a righteous foundation of peace.

I. First of all, then, it must never be forgotten that the Allies and America were forced to enter this war as a work of righteousness in order to make the world safe for peace.

Peace means something more than the mere absence of hostilities. It means justice, honour, fair-play, order, security, and the well-protected right of every man and nation to life, liberty, and the pursuit of happiness. It was the German contempt for these Christian ideals, it was the German idolatry of the pagan Odin, naked, cruel, bloody, god of war, it was the German will to power and dream of world-dominion, that made the world unsafe for real peace in 1914.

Never could that safety be secured until that enemy of mankind was overcome. Not only for democracy, but also for human peace, it was necessary, as President Wilson said, that "the German power, a thing without honour, conscience, or capacity for covenanted faith, must be crushed."

I saw, from my post of observation in Holland, the hosts of heathen Germany massing for their attack on the world's peace in the spring of 1914. Long before the pretext of war was provided by the murder of the Austrian Crown-Prince in Serajevo, I saw the troops, the artillery, the mountains of ammunition, assembled at Aix-la-Chapelle and Trier, ready for the invasion of neutral Belgium and Luxembourg, and the foul stroke at France.

Every civilized nation in Europe desired peace and pleaded for it. Little Servia offered to go before the Court of Arbitration at The Hague and be tried for the offense of which she was accused. Russia, Italy, France and England entreated Germany not to make war, but to submit the dispute to judicial settlement, to a righteous decision by a conference of powers. But Germany said no. She had prepared for war, she wanted war, she got war. And now she must abide by the result of her choice.

I have seen also with my own eyes the horrors wrought by Germany in her conduct of the war in Belgium and Northern France. Words fail me to describe them. Childhood has been crucified, womanhood outraged, civilization trampled in the dust. The nations and the men who took arms against these deviltries were the servants of the righteous God and the followers of the merciful Christ.

He told us, "If any man smite thee on the right cheek, turn unto him the left also." But never did He tell us to abandon the bodies and the lives of our women and children to the outrage of beasts in human form. On the contrary, He said to His disciples, in His parting discourse, "He that hath no sword let him sell his garment and buy one."

Does any silly pacifist say that means a spiritual sword? No. You could get that without selling your garment. It means a real sword,—as real as the purse and the scrip which Christ told His followers to carry with them. It means the power of arms dedicated to the service of righteousness without which the world can never be safe for peace.

Here, then, we may stand on the Word of God, on the work of righteousness in making the world safe for peace. Let me tell you of my faith that every one who has given his life for that cause, has entered into eternal rest.

II. Come we now to consider the second part of the text: "the effect of righteousness, quietness and confidence forever."

What shall be the nature of the peace to be concluded after our victory in this righteous war?

Here we have to oppose the demands of the bloodthirsty civilians. They ask that German towns should endure the same sufferings which have been inflicted on the towns of Belgium and Northern France. Let me say frankly that I do not believe you could persuade our officers to order such atrocities, or our soldiers to obey such orders. Read the order which one of the noble warriors of France, General Pétain, issued to his men:

"To-morrow, in order to better dictate peace, you are going to carry your arms as far as the Rhine. Into that land of Alsace-Lorraine that is so dear to us, you will march as liberators. You will go further; all the way into Germany to occupy lands which are the necessary guarantees for just reparation.

"France has suffered in her ravaged fields and in her ruined villages. The freed provinces have had to submit to intolerable vexations and odious outrages, but you are not to answer these crimes by the commission of violences, which, under the spur of your resentment, may seem to you legitimate.

"You are to remain under discipline and to show respect to persons and property. You will know, after having vanquished your adversary by force of arms, how to impress him further by the dignity of your attitude, and the world will not know which to admire most, your conduct in success or your heroism in fighting."

The destruction of the commonplace Cathedral of Cologne could never recompense the damage done to the glorious Cathedral of Rheims. Nor could the slaughter of a million German women and children restore the innocent victims of Belgium, France, Servia, and Armenia to life. We do not thirst for blood. We desire justice.

No doubt the ends of justice demand that the principal brigands who are responsible for the atrocities of this war should be tried before an international court If convicted they should be duly punished. But not by mob-law or violence. Nothing could be less desirable than the assassination of William Hohenzollern. It would be absurd and horrible to give a martyr's crown to a criminal. Vengeance belongeth unto God. He alone is wise and great enough to deal adequately with the case. It is for us to keep our righteous indignation free from the poison of personal hatred, and to do no more than is needed to uphold and vindicate the eternal law.

William Hohenzollern, and his fellow-conspirators who are responsible for the beginning and the conduct of the dreadful war from which all the toiling peoples of earth have suffered, must be brought to the bar of justice and sentenced; otherwise the world will have no defense against the anarchists who say that government is a vain thing; and the bloody Bolshevists who proclaim the Empire of the Ignorant,—the Boob-Rah,—as the future rule of the world, will have free scope.

It is evident that a league of free, democratic states, pledged by mutual covenant to uphold the settlement of international differences by reason and justice before the use of violence, offers the only hope of a durable peace among the nations. It is also the only defense against that deadly and destructive war of classes with which Bolshevism threatens the whole world. The spirit of Bolshevism is atheism and enmity; its method is violence and tyranny; its result would be a reign of terror under that empty-headed monster, "the dictatorship of the proletariat." God save us from that! It would be the worst possible outcome of the war in which we have offered and sacrificed so much, and in which God has given us the opportunity to make "a covenant of peace."

How vast, how immeasurable, are the responsibilities which this great victory in righteous war has laid upon the Allies and America. God help us to live up to them. God help us to sow the future not with dragon's teeth, but with seeds of blessed harvest. God paint upon the broken storm-cloud the rainbow of eternal hope. God help us and our friends to make a peace that shall mean good to all mankind. God send upon our victory the light of the cross of Christ our Saviour, where mercy and truth meet together, righteousness and peace kiss each other.

III

The Power of an Endless Life

Who is made, not after the law of a carnal commandment, but after the power of an endless life.—Hebrews 7:16.

---

he message and hope of immortality are nowhere more distinctly conveyed to our minds than in connection with that resurrection morn when Jesus appeared to Mary Magdalene. The anniversary of that day will ever be the festival of the human soul. Even those who do not clearly understand or fully accept its meaning in history and religion,—even children and ignorant folk and doubters and unbelievers,—yes, even frivolous people and sullen people, feel that there is something in this festival which meets the need and longing of their hearts. It is a day of joy and gladness, a day of liberation and promise, a day for flowers to bloom and birds to sing, a day of spiritual spring-tide and immortal hope.

Mankind desires and needs such a day. We are overshadowed in all our affections and aspirations, all our efforts, and designs, by the dark mystery of bodily death; the uncertainty and the brevity of earthly existence make us tremble and despair; the futility of our plans dismays us; the insecurity of our dearest treasure in lives linked to ours fills us with dismay.

Is there no escape from Death, the Tyrant, the autocrat, the destroyer, the last enemy? Why love, why look upward, why strive for better things if this imperator of failure, ultimate extinction, rules the universe? No hope beyond the grave means no peace this side of it. A life without hope is a life without God. If Death ends all, then there is no Father in Heaven in whom we can trust. Who shall deliver us from the body of this Death?

Now comes Easter with its immortal promise and assurance, Jesus of Nazareth, who died on Calvary, a martyr of humanity, a sacrifice of Divinity, is alive and appears to His humble followers. The manner of His appearance, to Mary Magdalene, to His disciples, is not the most important thing. The fact is that He did appear. He who was crucified in the cause of righteousness and mercy, lives on and forever. The message of His resurrection is "the power of an endless life."

The proof of this message is in the effect that it produced. It transformed the handful of Jesus' followers from despair to confidence. It gave Christianity its growing influence over the heart of humanity. It is this message of immortality that makes religion vital to the human world to-day, and essential to the foundation of peace on earth.

We must not forget in our personal griefs and longings, in our sorrows for those whom we have lost and our desire to find them again, in our sense of our own mortal frailty and the brief duration of earthly life, the celestial impulse which demands a life triumphant over death.

The strongest of all supports for peace on earth is the faith in immortality. The truth is, the very character of our being here in this world demands continuance beyond death. There is nothing good or great that we think or feel or endeavour, that is not a reaching out to something better. Our finest knowledge is but the consciousness of limitation and the longing that it may be removed. Our best moral effort is but a slow advance towards something better. Our sense of the difference between good and evil, our penitence, our aspiration, all this moral freight with which our souls are laden, is a cargo consigned to an unseen country. Our bill of lading reads, "To the immortal life." If we must sink in mid-ocean, then all is lost, and the voyage of life is a predestined wreck.

The wisest, the strongest, the best of mankind, have felt this most deeply. The faith in immortality belongs to the childhood of the race, and the greatest of the sages have always returned to it and taken refuge in it. Socrates and Plato, Cicero and Plutarch, Montesquieu and Franklin, Kant and Emerson, Tennyson and Browning,—how do they all bear witness to the incompleteness of life and reach out to a completion beyond the grave.

"No great Thinker ever lived and taught you All the wonder that his soul received; No great Painter ever set on canvas All the glorious vision he conceived.

"No Musician ever held your spirit Charmed and bound in his melodious chains; But, be sure, he heard, and strove to render, Feeble echoes of celestial strains.

"No real Poet ever wove in numbers All his dream, but the diviner part, Hidden from all the world, spake to him only In the voiceless silence of his heart.

"So with Love: for Love and Art united Are twin mysteries: different yet the same; Poor indeed would be the love of any Who could find its full and perfect name.

"Love may strive; but vain is its endeavour All its boundless riches to unfold; Still its tenderest, truest secret lingers Ever in its deepest depths untold.

"Things of Time have voices: speak and perish. Art and Love speak; but their words must be Like sighings of illimitable forests And waves of an unfathomable sea."

And can it be that death shall put the final seal of irretrievable ruin on all this uncompleted effort? Can it be that the grave shall whelm all this unuttered love in endless silence? Ah, what a wild waste of precious treasure, what a mad destruction of fair designs, what an utter failure, life would be if death must end all!

The very reasonableness of our nature, our sense of order, declare the impotence of Death to create such a wreck. And most of all our deep affections cry out against the conclusion of despair. They will not hear of dissolution. They reach out their hands into the darkness. They demand and they promise an unending fellowship, a deepening communion, a more perfect satisfaction. Do you remember what Thackeray wrote? "If love lives through all life, and survives through all sorrow; and remains steadfast with us through all changes; and in all darkness of spirit burns brightly; and if we die, deplores us forever, and still loves us equally; and exists with the very last gasp and throb of the faithful bosom, whence it passes with the pure soul beyond death, surely it shall be immortal. Though we who remain are separated from it, is it not ours in heaven? If we love still those whom we lose, can we altogether lose those whom we love?"

To deny this instinct is to deny that which lies at the very root of our life. If love perishes with death, then our affections are our worst curses, the world is the cruellest torture-house, and "all things work together for evil to those who love." Do you believe it? Is it possible? Nay, all that is best and noblest and purest within us rejects such a faith in Absolute Evil as the power that has created and rules the world. In the presence of love we feel that we behold that which must belong to a good God and therefore cannot die. Destruction cannot touch it. The grave cannot hold it. Loving and being loved, we dare to stand in the very doorway of the tomb, and assert the power of an endless life.

And it seems to me that this courage never comes to us so fully as when we are brought in closest contact with death, when we are brought face to face with that dread shadow and forced either to deny its power, once and forever, or to give up everything and die with our hopes. I wish that I could make this clear to you as it lies in my own experience. Perhaps in trying to do it I should speak closer to your own heart than in any other way. For surely

"There is no flock, however watched and tended But one dead lamb is there. There is no fireside, howsoe'er defended But has a vacant chair."

A flower grew in your garden. You delighted in its beauty and fragrance. It gave you all it had to give, but it did not love you. It could not. When the time came for it to die, you were sorry. But it did not seem to you strange or unnatural. There was no waste. Its mission was fulfilled. You understood why its petals should fall, its leaf wither, its root and branch decay. And even if a storm came and snapped it, still there was nothing lost that was indispensable, nothing that could not be restored.

A child grew in your household, dearly loved and answering your love. You saw that soul unfold, learning to know the evil from the good, learning to accept duty and to resist selfishness, learning to be brave and true and kind, learning to give you day by day a deeper and a richer sympathy, learning to love God and to pray and to be good. And then perhaps you saw that young heart being perfected under the higher and holier discipline of suffering, bearing pain patiently, facing trouble and danger like a hero, not shrinking even from the presence of death, but trusting all to your love and to God's, and taking just what came from day to day, from hour to hour. And then suddenly the light went out in the shining eyes. The brave heart stopped. The soul was gone. Lost, perished, blotted out forever in the darkness of death? Ah, no; you know better than that. That clear, dawning intelligence, that deepening love, that childlike faith in God, that pure innocence of soul, did not come from the dust. How could they return thither? The music ceases because the instrument is broken. But the player is not dead. He is learning a better music. He is finding a more perfect

18

instrument. It is impossible that he should be holden of death. God wastes nothing so precious.

"What is excellent As God lives is permanent. Hearts are dust; hearts' loves remain. Hearts' love will meet thee again."

But I am sure that we must go further than this in order to understand the full strength and comfort of the text. The assertion of the impotence of death to end all is based upon something deeper than the prophecy of immortality in the human heart. It has a stronger foundation than the outreachings of human knowledge and moral effort towards a higher state in which completion may be attained. It has a more secure ground to rest upon than the deathless affection with which our love clings to its object The impotence of death is revealed to us in the spiritual perfection of Christ.

Here then, in the "power of an endless life," I find the corner-stone of peace on earth among men of good-will Take this mortal life as a thing of seventy years, more or less, to which death puts a final period, and you have nothing but confusion, chance and futility,— nothing safe, nothing realized, nothing completed. Evil often triumphs. Virtue often is defeated.

"The good die young, And we whose hearts are dry as summer dust Burn to the socket."

But take death, as Christ teaches us, not as a full stop, but as only a comma in the story of an endless life, and then the whole aspect of our existence is changed. That which is material, base, evil, drops down. That which is spiritual, noble, good, rises to lead us on.

The conviction of immortality, the forward-looking faith in a life beyond the grave, the spirit of Easter, is essential to peace on earth for three reasons.

I. It is the only faith that lifts man's soul, which is immortal, above his body, which is perishable. It raises him out of the tyranny of the flesh to the service of his ideals. It makes him sure that there are things worth fighting and dying for. The fighting and the dying, for the cause of justice and liberty, are sacrifices on the Divine altar which shall never be forgotten.

II. The faith in immortality carries with it the assurance of a Divine reassessment of earth's inequalities. Those who have suffered unjustly here will be recompensed in the future. Those who have acted wickedly and unjustly here will be punished. Whether that punishment will be final or remedial we do not know. Perhaps it may lead to the extinction of the soul of evil, perhaps to its purifying and deliverance. On these questions I fall back on the word of God: "The wages of sin is death, but the gift of God is eternal life in Christ Jesus our Lord."

III. The faith in immortality brings with it the sense of order, tranquillity, steadiness and courage in the present life. It sets us free from mean and cowardly temptations, makes it easier to resist the wild animal passions of lust and greed and cruelty, brings us into eternal relations and fellowships, makes us partners with the wise and good of all the ages, ennobles our earthly patriotism by giving us a heavenly citizenship. Yea, it knits us in bonds of love with the coming generation. It is better than the fountain of youth. We shall know and see them as they go on their way, long after we have left the path. The faith in immortality sets a touch of the imperishable on every generous impulse and unselfish deed. It inspires to sublime and heroic virtues,—spiritual splendours,— deeds of sacrifice and suffering for which earth has no adequate recompense, but whose reward is great in heaven. Here is the patience of the saints, the glorious courage of patriots, martyrs, and confessors, something more bright and shining than secular morality can bring forth,—a flashing of the inward light which fails not, but grows clearer as death draws near. What noble evidences of this come to us out of the great war.

"Are you in great distress?" asked a nurse of an American soldier whose legs had been shot away on the battle-field. "I am in as great peace," said he, "through Jesus my Lord, as a man can possibly be, out of Paradise."

A secretary of the Y.M.C.A., the night before he was killed, wrote to his father: "I have not been sent here to die: I am to fight: I offer my life for future generations; I shall not die, I shall merely change my direction. He who walks before us is so great that we cannot lose Him from sight."

A simple French boy, grievously wounded, is dying in the ambulance. He is a Protestant The nurse who bends over him is a Catholic sister. She writes down his words as they fall slowly from his lips: "O my God, let Thy will be done and not mine. O my God, Thou knowest that I never wished war, but that I have fought because it was Thy will; I offered my life so that peace might prevail. O my God, I pray for all my dear ones, ... father, mother, brothers, sisters. Give a hundredfold to those nurses for all they have done for me. I pray for them one and all."

Here, in the midst of carnage and confusion, horror and death, was perfect peace, the triumph of immortality.

What then shall we say of the new teachers and masters, the cynical lords of materialism and misrule, who tell us that they are going to banish this outworn superstition and all others like it from the mind of man? They are going to make a new world in which men shall walk by sight, and not by faith; a world in which universal happiness shall be produced by the forcible division of material goods, and brotherhood promoted by the simple expedient of killing those whom they dislike; a world in which there shall be neither nation, God, nor Church, nor anywhere a thought of any life but this which ends in the grave. It is a mad dream of wild and reckless men. But it threatens evil to all the world. Do you remember what happened when the French Revolution took that course, abolished the Sabbath, defiled the Churches, broke down the altars, and enthroned a harlot as the Goddess of Reason? The Reign of Terror followed. Something like that has happened, recently, in many parts of Europe. And if these new tyrants of ignorance, unbelief, and unmorality have their way, the madness and the darkness will spread until the black cloud charged with death covers the face of the earth for a season with shame and anguish and destruction. A sane world, an orderly world, a peaceful world, can never be founded on materialism. That foundation is a quicksand in which all that is dearest to man goes down in death.

Religion is essential to true peace in the soul and to peace on earth through righteousness. Immortality is essential to true religion. Thanks be to God who hath given us Jesus Christ, who was dead and is alive again and liveth forevermore, to touch and ennoble, to inspire and console, to pacify and uplift our earthly existence with the power of an endless life.

Printed in Great Britain
by Amazon.co.uk, Ltd.,
Marston Gate.